D0672501

TROUT CHASER'S
JOURNAL

A Diary for the Trout & Salmon Fisherman

By Tully Stroud

Chronicle Books, San Francisco

ACKNOWLEDGMENTS

The small but vengeful group of my close fishing companions has threatened reprisal if identified in this work. I wanted to thank them. Not for their support—they laughed uproariously at the idea of my writing a book about trout fishing before I had demonstrated an ability to catch one—but for the many good times we've shared chasing trout. My attorney says that since they are self-admitted fishermen, they are, by definition, incapable of mounting a credible defense and can be defamed with total impunity. Thanks then to my brother Dennis, Jim Coultas, Preston Plumb, Jim Nelson, and Dennis Byrne. Thanks also to my sons Jim and Padraic who have (for better or worse) come to share my love for the sport and have, to date at least, shown humility on those increasingly frequent occasions when they outfish their father.

I extend special thanks to another group—the superb outdoor photographers published in this book, whose images capture the spirit of trout fishing far better than my words ever could. To a mother and father who chose to spend family vacations on trout streams instead of under palm trees, I can't thank you enough. And, to Don McQuiston, Debra McQuiston, and Frankie Wright—thanks for teaming up to produce this book and to translate my words into something roughly resembling the English language.

Cover photo: Fisherman with British Columbia Steelhead (Salmo gairdneri) *by Jim Vincent*

All rights reserved. No part of this book may be reproduced in any form without written permission from the publisher.

Printed and bound by Mandarin Offset Marketing (H.K.) Ltd., through Interprint, San Francisco

Produced and designed by McQuiston & Daughter, Del Mar, California Edited by Frankie Wright

Mechanical production by Curt Boyer Composition by Thompson Type, San Diego

ISBN: 0-87701-404-3

Chronicle Books One Hallidie Plaza San Francisco, California 94102

10 9 8 7 6 5 4 3 2 1

For Patricia
whose tolerance and understanding of my affair with trout long ago surpassed mortal limits and earned her the sympathy of all who know her.

Tom Montgomery

Snake River, Grand Teton National Park, Wyoming by Pat O'Hara

PROLOGUE

Man will always seek escapes—special places where troubles are forgotten. Some folks seek the sea or the high country. Others retreat to ski slopes or wine cellars. But for a few of us, the ultimate escape is to find a stream somewhere and try to outwit a trout.

The tonic effects of a stream are really quite magical. We're mesmerized into a state of alert calm. We're spellbound and cannot escape. Streams, whether large rivers or small creeks, are almost invariably beautiful and run their course through beautiful places. They may flow through forests, canyons, meadows, or sagebrush flats. They may meander gently or tumble violently. Currents cascading through subtle blends of sunlight and shadow melt our defenses against serenity. Eventually, we must surrender.

Our senses are teased by scents—pine trees, wet leaves, or sage—that liberate our memories, sending us back to a time when life somehow seemed less complicated, to a pleasant place filled with agreeable things and congenial people.

And beyond the melodies of birds and the calming rush of wind is that wonderfully hypnotic white noise of the river itself. Ever present, yet somehow invisible, noise drowns out what is left of an unwanted outside world and brings us deeper into the trance of the stream.

Sadly, few of us can live out our lives in such a trance. We visit streams only briefly, then trek back into a peopled world of economic and social pressures, into a world that looks askance at people who don't or won't fit in. After listening to friends tell stories about their ski trips to Colorado or marathons in Boston, we are reluctant to tell them that our idea of fun is simply sitting on some streambank listening to a river gurgle! Clearly, a cover is needed to stave off those strange looks. Trout and salmon fishing provides the perfect excuse. Not only is it socially acceptable, it's actually great fun. Even better, these fish are nearly always found in the very setting we seek.

But be warned! Trout fishing can become an all-consuming passion and one which, if permitted to blossom unrestrained, can become a not-so-benign addiction. Over-indulgence can cause reason to dim, perspective to warp, and all remnants of what the rest of the world calls sanity to vanish.

Beyond its clear and present threat to our willing acceptance of life back home, fishing can also become a *financial* black hole. The sport is subject to the same collecting mania that inflicts so many other hobbies, and the collectibles aren't cheap. But the limitless paraphernalia is just the tip of the proverbial iceberg. A far greater threat is the faraway places trout chasing can take us. Some superb fishing is found these days in the general vicinity of such well-known vacation hot spots as San Carlos de Bariloche in Argentina, Te Anau in New Zealand, Afjord in Norway, Llifen in Chile, and Iliamna in our own Alaskan bush. At last check, airline fare wars—and in some cases, airlines themselves—had not yet reached these towns, and the fishing lodge fees (although a psychic bargain) are generally not what most of us would call cheap. One fine purveyor of fishing trips, for example, has offered a dream trip of about sixty days to a few of the South American trout meccas for "approximately $20,000." If the "approximately" causes you to pause, don't bother to inquire about the additional cost of getting to Argentina and back.

Thankfully, trout of some variety are found in nearly all of the fifty states, so the sport can easily be pursued with relative sanity and

"Trout fishing can become an all-consuming passion and one which, if permitted to blossom unrestrained, can become a not-so-benign addiction. Over-indulgence can cause reason to dim, perspective to warp . . ."

frugality much closer to home. Wilderness areas that have been preserved forever in our national and state parks and forests (as well as in vast Forest Service holdings) offer an array of fishing opportunities. These legacies give the United States the widest selection of affordable, publicly accessible trout and salmon fishing to be found anywhere on the planet.

We can't grow complacent with what we have, however. Battles of vital concern to the fisherman—acid rain, habitat (especially spawning habitat) destruction, and direct pollution, to name but a few—are far from over.

Neither is all doom and gloom. Some of our "wild" rivers have now been set aside to remain that way. Polluted rivers and lakes are being reborn as we make dramatic progress in cleaning up many of our past mistakes. Wild trout programs continue to prove that, given the right aquatic environment, fisheries can be self-sustaining and thrive without expensive manmade hatcheries to help out. Where dams or other impediments have made natural spawning impossible, steelhead and salmon populations have been preserved by well-conceived hatchery programs. Stricter catch limits, special regulations setting minimum or maximum sizes for fish kept, and the growing popularity of catch-and-release fishing continue to reduce the heavy strain on our limited supply of fish.

Important struggles to preserve trout and their habitat continue to be fought with fervor. A clear fact seems to have already emerged from the fray: *All* of us care about preserving the kind of environment in which a trout can live. It is a caring born of appreciation for the quality these places bring to our lives. And a caring spawned by more than a little guilt at all we have destroyed by treating Nature as a commodity for our use, rather than as a complex community of which we are only a part. When this evolution of understanding is complete, the future of the trout—and perhaps man himself—will be secure.

Opening Day, Box Canyon, Henry's Fork of the Snake River, Idaho by Terry Ring

SPRING

An early spring fishing trip, especially an opening day trip, is often more enjoyable if viewed as a humorous study in abnormal human behavior than as a real fishing experience. It is virtually impossible to overestimate the determination of the trout fisherman who has been cooped up in the house all winter wishing he were fishing. The extremes to which he may go defy understanding. To anyone but another trout fisherman, that is.

Consider, if you will, a fairly typical, thrill-packed day for an early season trout fisherman:

4:00 A.M. Because he is too cheap ("rugged," he'll tell you) to pop for a motel room, he shivers inside a frost-covered sleeping bag, agonizing over whether to brave hypothermia and try some early fishing or to wait for the sun to warm the water and him along with it.

5:15 A.M. The agony continues. If he can just feign sleep long enough, one of this buddies will weaken first. The painful legacy of liquid refreshment the night before generally dictates that the one with the smallest bladder wins the "first up" honors.

5:28 A.M. Because he is the lucky winner (again), he dons thermal underwear, layers of socks, mittens, boots, and a parka, and finally emerges from the toasty cocoon to fumble with wet wood and shaky fingers to build a fire.

5:52 A.M. Sipping coffee he would spit out at home, he sits beside the life-giving fire and brushes tears from smoke-filled eyes. Knowing this is the last bit of comfort for a long while, he savors it. The ice in his hair slowly melts.

6:08 A.M. After stalling for as long as possible, he slips into frozen waders and gallantly heads through the snow for the stream.

6:22 A.M. He finds a gap in the long line of fishermen cursed with even smaller bladders and wades into the water. There, he stands on legs too numb to walk. With each cast, he dips his rod into the water to melt ice from the guides.

7:08 A.M. After casting in a carefully timed manner for a near-record 46 minutes, he finally breaks the rhythm. He spends the next ten minutes trying, with frozen fingers, to untangle the resulting snarl of lines, followed by another ten minutes trying to tie any kind of a knot that will join a leader and a hook.

8:42 A.M. He finally lands a fish (and three other lines as well). Whether or not he releases it or takes it back for lunch, he'll have to get his hands wet.

9:21 A.M. His hands having taken the plunge, he has two choices. Both are bad. He must either continue to dip his frozen fingers into the river to thaw them out or find a warm spot somewhere beneath his waders. He opts for the latter, gets strange looks from the spectators, and parents start hiding their children.

11:46 A.M. Using lunch as an excuse, he returns to camp, basks in the warmth of a fire, chats awhile with his pals about how great it was, and stretches out for a nap. But guilt keeps him awake.

1:25 P.M. Back on the river, he looks up from his concentrated casting long enough to notice that the sky now resembles the screen of a 1949 television set experiencing technical difficulties. The snow, of course, is propelled by the usual 25-knot swirling wind, and the driven flakes gather in drifts inside his parka hood. He feels icy water dripping down his back. He'd like to change the channel.

3:21 P.M. The lunchtime coffee issues an ultimatum and he heads painfully toward shore. This is not a junket to be undertaken lightly or accomplished quickly under even the best of conditions. Technology has been directed toward things like cameras that talk, at the expense of such low tech needs as waders with a fly (not the fishing variety) in them.

6:09 P.M. With a clear conscience born of knowing that he has dutifully served the full term of his opening day sentence, he reels in his line, puts the fly in the hook keeper and turns to head his numb body for shore. He takes two labored steps before he trips over a rock and falls in up to his neck.

6:17 P.M. He reaches camp in the early stages of hypothermia and seeks to avoid embarrassment before the group by telling the others that he slipped while pursuing a tuna-sized trout down the river.

6:25 P.M. Another member of the party arrives equally drenched, claiming that he too was towed toward the horizon by a great trout.

7:38 P.M. After much telling and re-telling of the day's events by each member of the group, the conclusion is unanimous: The hooking of two such large fish at the end of the day indicates that the fish are "going on the feed" and tomorrow should be great. Nodding agreement, he bolts down the last of his canned stew and heads for his sleeping bag muttering something about taking up bonefish chasing in the Bahamas.

Why would a creature with an I.Q. any higher than that of a slab of cement voluntarily subject himself to this kind of punishment and think it entertaining? All gray-bearded fishermen finally come to realize that the early spring trip, like the essence of the sport itself, really has less to do with the act of fishing than with camaraderie. It's the annual renewal of old friendships born of a strong, common bond. These relationships grow over the course of a lifetime, and the older we get, the more we cherish them.

Seldom, in the course of the year, can we gather all or even most of our fishing friends together for one grand trip. Careers and the inertia of everyday life warp our perspective of the *truly* important things and conspire to keep us apart and away from the stream. Fortunately, with every spring comes the perfect excuse. Opening day!

Never mind that many states now have year-round trout seasons. Any fishing addict worth his waders will still find an opening day *somewhere*! If everyone can't be gathered together for the opener, no matter. Any long weekend thereabouts will do just fine. Just be sure and take along a bedpan and your sense of humor.

Michigan Spring by Larry Dech

THE TEACHER

His name was Tick Lane, and he was a barber. Not a hairstylist, but an old-fashioned barber with a shaving mug and a heavy hand on the shears and lilac water. He was also a fisherman of the most dedicated variety and a man of absolutely Jobaic patience. For three long summers, he spent his free Mondays teaching an eager, if somewhat inept, youngster to fly-fish for trout. It was a monumental undertaking, but by the end of that third summer, the trout finally began outnumbering the wind knots.

Nearly everyone who calls himself a trout fisherman has someone to thank. Thanks to all you patient tutors whose only reward comes in watching your pupil take his first trout on a fly. Thanks to that ancient Greek who first put a feather on a hook and started it all. And, by the way, thanks to you too, Tick.

Pink Floyd by R. Valentine Atkinson

PINK FLOYD

Fishing was slow, and Jim was frustrated.

"I'm done throwing all that delicate stuff at 'em," he proclaimed. "Those fish are just plain bored, and I'm going to tie up something that'll get their hearts pounding."

He did. A monster of a streamer with an oversized tail and wings of gawdy pink marabou. The whole thing looked more like fare for a colorblind tarpon than a trout fly.

"There it is," he declared proudly. "Pink Floyd. A killer!"

Many past meals of unplucked crow should have taught the rest of us not to laugh at Jim's offbeat ideas, but the way the silly thing looked, we just couldn't help it.

Later that afternoon, a brown trout, which Jim and an allegedly unpaid witness swore weighed over 10 pounds, mistook Pink Floyd for God-only-knows-what and tried to either kill it or mate with it.

After a mighty struggle, Jim lost that fish of a lifetime. But he did land a couple of chubby three pounders on that trip with his ugly fly, while the rest of us caught the big donut.

It was a fluke. I know it was a fluke. But just to be sure, you can bet I now own enough pink marabou to outfit every chorus girl in Las Vegas.

His First Trout by Larry Dech

FIRST TROUT

Our first trout is immortal. It lives forever in one of those special chambers in our memories reserved for the likes of first loves.

Fishermen on Northern California Ranch by
R. Valentine Atkinson

THE FISHING TRIP

Most fishermen deal with their trout-chasing afflictions by forming self-help groups with others of similar financial and social constraints. Such therapy groups meet several times a year on what are generally known as "fishing trips." On these occasions, group members reinforce their valid but fragile conviction that it is *they* who have things in perspective and the rest of the world is out of touch.

Fishing Hat by R. Valentine Atkinson

HATS

Felt hats . . . leather hats … wool hats … baseball caps. No two are alike, and they are probably the most personal item in the fisherman's trunk of angling garb. The older and more ragged they become, the better they are and the more we love them.

Parting with a well-seasoned hat, whether through loss or eventual disintegration, is a real trauma. That miserably uncomfortable breaking-in of a new one has to be endured. New hats are always too stiff, too clean, never fit right, and attract attention of the variety that can earn the brand of "dude."

When I was much younger and more naive, I once made the mistake of wearing a brand new black Stetson into a Montana saloon. My buddies and I hadn't even ordered a cool one before a friendly local at the other end of the bar opened the conversation with: "Say, just what part of California you boys from?"

When we walked out a little later, one of my friends took off my Stetson and threw it onto the ground, whereupon the other chum jumped on it until it was flat. The hat looked better immediately. I now throw any new hat into the dirt and walk on it a few times just to give it a good headstart. Californians are proud people, but for reasons well-known to Texans and New Yorkers, we prefer to keep our origins anonymous.

Soleduck River, Olympic National Park, Washington by Pat O'Hara

CONTEMPLATION
Sometimes, rivers and the lands that surround them are so overwhelming to the senses that even the most avid fisherman comes upon a moment when he must put down his rod, sit on a rock, and just look at it all in awe.

Silver Creek, Idaho by David Stoecklein

REFLECTIONS

My earliest memories are of streams. Timeless rivers full of fish. The hot summer day when a lad of four watched, with awe and pride, as his father caught a bass from a small creek in Arkansas. The morning when an 8-year-old flipped his lure through the eerie morning mist and into the green waters of California's Eel River to catch his first trout. The boy of ten catching another first—a strapping 13-inch brown from Wyoming's Green River while, this time, his father looked on with pride.

Once in a while, in quiet times, I plan a sentimental journey back to those Edens of my youth. Though Dad can't make the trip this time, he'll be there just the same. Rivers are like that.

Sunset on the Salmon River, Idaho by David Stoecklein

SIMPLICITY
If you require much more than this to be happy, you've probably picked up this book by mistake.

Nushagak River, Alaska by Kitty Pearson-Vincent

SUMMER

After shivering in ice water throughout the short and frigid days of spring, the trout fisherman is more than ready for the great thaw that comes with summer. It isn't that summer fishing is better. The trout aren't half so gullible as they are in early spring. And it sure as heck isn't that the streams are less crowded. That'll have to wait for the falling leaves of autumn. No, it's those long, warm summer days of wearing sunscreen and T-shirts instead of balaclavas and goosedown ... of swatting bugs instead of dodging ice floes ... of chugging cold beers in the hot sun instead of sipping warm brandy through blue lips.

The more hours of daylight, the better. A summer day, even in southern climes, can have a good sixteen hours of fishable light. And the farther north one goes the better it has to get. Now, if a fisherman were to go far enough north, he could actually find the utopian fishing day. Twenty-four hours of light. Think of it! No downtime. Around-the-clock entertainment. Paradise without the distraction of Eve.

A few years ago, I decided to seek out this fisherman's paradise and headed off alone for the land of the midnight sun. I rolled the old pickup off the ferry in Haynes, Alaska on the very day of the summer solstice and hit the road for trout and salmon country. Ahead lay a whole summer of fishing every hot spot in the Last Frontier, wherever roads and float planes could take me and that my relatively modest budget could support. Ten weeks later, I rolled the old pickup back onto the ferry in Haynes—a stammering, stumbling, incoherent wreck of a man.

It didn't take long to discover that, without the external discipline imposed by darkness, I was in real trouble. This Eden had an abundance of apples, and my resistance to temptation was somewhere around nonexistent. With all the zeal of a freed prisoner, I fished for rainbow trout, sockeye salmon, grayling, Dolly Varden, and even mighty king salmon throughout the eerie gray glow of the subarctic night. I'd grab a quick breakfast of granola bars and coffee, and head back to the stream for daytime fishing. Then back to camp for a fast dinner of barbequed sockeye and two or three hours of sleep before the long night of fishing ahead.

By the third day, I was stumbling in the stream. By the fourth day, my speech was slurred. By the fifth day, I got lost on my way to the river—a trip that was all of three hundred yards along a trail as deeply rutted as the Burma Road. Then things started to get serious. I began missing strikes and losing fish. Somewhere around day seven, the unthinkable actually happened. I got tired of catching big fish and, in moments when I could think at all, started longing for Eve instead. Something had gone radically wrong in paradise.

Looking back on that trip, the lesson is clear. It is indeed possible to have too much of a good thing—even fishing. Prolonged indulgence only loosens the poor fisherman's already slippery hold on sanity. Ten weeks is definitely too long. *Six* weeks would be about perfect!

On that trip, I was alone much of the time. Not only was there no wife to share all the fun, but there was nobody to wager with, nobody to plan the next day with, nobody to share stories or swap lies with. I got plain lonesome.

Solos are refreshing occasionally, but fishing is a sport founded in the careful mix of companionship and solitude. A fish caught alone can be much like the tree falling noiselessly in the empty woods. We need *people* to share the experiences with, to laugh with (and at), and to help with meals, dishes, and gas money.

"It is indeed possible to have too much of a good thing—even fishing. Prolonged indulgence only loosens the poor fisherman's already slippery hold on sanity."

What does all this idle rambling about the trout fisherman's need for company have to do with summer? Plenty. Summer, you see, is just about the only time we can arrange that eagerly anticipated time of quality togetherness— *the family fishing trip*!

Summer is the time to sidestep those boring trips other families take and do what we know they really yearn for—*fish*! After all, who in their right mind would prefer snorkeling in Tahiti to busting brush and swatting mosquitoes on the Beaverhead? Who indeed. Would anyone really rather see Paris than join a loved one for a long, cold day of summer steelhead fishing in a driving rain on the Soleduck? Nobody I'd share a roof with.

Every summer then, it's the family fisherman's duty to devote one or more weeks to letting the rest of the family share in the fun. Such family outings are nearly always unifying, for better or for worse. Improperly executed, they can bind the group together with a common glue—abject misery. Or done right, they can be the best of times.

After a relatively modest investment of time and attention, the fisherman will usually witness an amazing transformation. Family members become delightfully self-reliant and actually start to enjoy the fishing experience. Many even come to share our addiction. Luckily, no state yet recognizes this corruption as a crime.

Only by sacrificing some fishing time up front so that others will get hooked can the fisherman hope to reach that ultimate Eden of emotional well-being: *fishing without guilt*.

Alaskan Rainbow (Salmo gairdneri) *by Tom Montgomery*

COURTSHIP

Trout chasing is a form of courtship. When we aren't actively courting, we're daydreaming about it. When we're courting without success, it's a sweet hurt— a character builder that makes the eventual success all the sweeter. The chase must offer the prospect of success, but victory, any true victory, means a long and nervous period of wooing. One of the most surprising lessons I've learned in my rather undistinguished fishing career is that an easy victory is actually worse than a narrow defeat that leaves us aching for a rematch.

All my life, I had dreamed of catching big trout until my arm ached. Then, one day, my dreams came true on a small creek in Alaska. My very first cast produced a five pounder! Nearly every well-placed cast thereafter meant a hookup. The fish—rainbow trout—were all big, strong, and acrobatic, yet after a few were landed and released, I grew bored and began trying to shake off the three and four pounders. Then I lost interest in the five and six pounders. The courtship had turned into an orgy! I spent the afternoon just walking the banks looking in vain for the elusive "double digit" fish—the over ten pounder—that probably wasn't even there.

It was a sobering experience. Any *one* of those fish would normally have made a success of an entire fishing trip, but it was just too much too fast. Which creek you ask? Forget it. I said I was bored—not crazy.

*Atlantic Salmon (*Salmo salar*) Laxa i Adaldal River, Iceland by Kris Lee*

THE ATLANTIC SALMON

"All kydells [fish-weirs] for the future shall be removed altogether from the Thames and Medway, and throughout all England..."

This dreamy sounding demand was not on the wish list of some British angling club. It carried a little more clout. The year was 1215, the scene was the meadow at Runnymede, and the document was the Magna Carta.

The rebellious barons were really out to preserve navigation rather than fish, but their Great Charter did buy a little time for the Atlantic salmon. When King John grudgingly applied the sealing wax at Runnymede, the Thames was still a respectable salmon stream, and some of the finest runs were in Germany's Rhine and Portugal's Duoro.

Unfortunately for the salmon, England did not speak for the rest of the world on the subject of dam building. And in the end, it probably mattered little anyway, for man's concern for the salmon was no match for the pressures of population and the Industrial Revolution. The last wild Atlantic salmon is said to have been caught in the Thames in 1833 and dined upon by the King, who paid a guinea a pound for the privilege. By that time, the great salmon runs of the Rhine, Duoro, Oder, Elbe, and many other European rivers, were already history. North America was busy enacting the same tragic history on the other side of the Atlantic.

Today, the Atlantic salmon holds on in a fraction of its former range while nations argue over appropriate ways to protect the fish from wholesale slaughter on its high-sea feeding grounds. Some progress has been made, but we need only look at the trend line of the salmon's numbers over the past seven centuries to remind ourselves that *Salmo salar* is still a good candidate for becoming but a fond memory.

*The Native Fisherman (*Ursus arctos*) by Tom Bean*

GRIZZLIES

Don't let them kid you for a minute. Fishermen who say they go to Alaska just to catch the big rainbow are no more after just the fish than rock climbers are merely after the summit view. No trip to Alaska could be complete without at least one spotting of *Ursus arctos*—the grizzly bear.

Grizzlies living along the Alaskan coast (still known to most of us as Alaskan brown bears) enjoy a diet so rich they can grow to immense sizes that dwarf their inland brothers. They spend the summer gorging themselves on spawning salmon in the same streams that host the big rainbows and the fishermen who chase them. (Fishermen are forever chasing rainbows.) There's something secretly exciting to us city folks about fishing with one eye on the water and the other scanning the landscape for the biggest carnivore that walks the earth.

If the intruding fisherman uses common sense and maintains the necessary high level of respect for the native fisherman, encounters are usually at a distance and harmful only to the nerves.

Henry's Fork of the Snake River, Idaho by Terry Ring

WHITEFISH

The green drake hatch on the Henry's Fork is an event that has to be seen to be believed. First, there are the green drakes themselves—giant green mayflies the size of small butterflies that clutter the air and litter the stream. Then there are the fish—big, built like watermelons and, at hatch time, gluttonous but still frustratingly picky. Finally, there are the fishermen. These guys are *serious*! On a June evening, there's enough fine angling paraphernalia in the roughly 9-mile meadow section of this river to grossly overstock every fishing tackle shop west of the Mississippi.

Before my first trip to this fishing Holy Land, I read all the lore on the subject. Long, light leaders. Flies that look more like the real thing than the real thing. Snaky, downstream casts. Stealth. Boy, was I ready.

Unfortunately, one small detail was omitted from all the "how to" scoop. If one doesn't know (or is too obtuse to learn) the difference between the rise of a rainbow trout and that of a whitefish, one will quickly learn the true meaning of abject frustration. Trout, you see, have nice big mouths that engulf an artificial fly with ease. Whitefish, on the other hand, try with great zeal to do the same but don't seem to have enough mouth to get the job done. Unfortunately, I learned that fact only after enduring both frustration *and* embarrassment in large doses.

After watching others catch giant rainbows while I missed strike after strike, I muttered, mumbled, and headed for shore. Turning to watch another angler play a large fish, I stumbled over the only rock in sight and went in up to my hat in front of half the trout fishermen in the civilized world. Alarmed, my wife stopped fishing and called out my *name* from 200 yards downstream. (She's got a mouth like a trout.) I know I've had more embarrassing moments, but they've been delightfully repressed.

Firehole River, Yellowstone National Park, Wyoming by R. Valentine Atkinson

SUMMER WADING

Even in this time of neoprene waders and polypropylene long johns, a few of us black sheep still secretly look forward to a hot summer day when we can throw the fruits of modern technology to the wind and go out and live a little on that ragged edge of danger called "wet wading."

To risk bruised knees or scraped ankles for the sake of a little cooling comfort has become unfashionable. So we sometimes slip—is there anyone out there who hasn't done the same in waders? Who cares if we have to walk ashore once in a while to thaw out our legs in the sun? When it's 103° in the shade and you could fry eggs on the river rocks, the rewards outweigh the inconveniences. So turn back the clock and live a little!

Solitude Along Alaskan Roadside by Tully Stroud

THE REDS ARE IN!

Somewhere around the summer solstice each year, the long-awaited word goes out over Alaskan radio, television, and newspapers: *The reds are in on the Russian River.*

The ensuing evacuation of the city of Anchorage should be the model for every civil defense agency in the world, because to all appearances, every man, woman, and child in the city hightails it to the first roadside salmon run of the year. The cure for cabin fever. On a weekend when the run is in full swing, you may wait in line just for a parking place near the river. Finding elbow room along the small stream is even tougher.

Fishing the Russian at such times is definitely not for the timid or the serious fisherman seeking seclusion. It's better viewed—preferably from a safe distance—as a show. Entertainment. Lines are tangled long before a fish enters the picture. When a red salmon (the local name for a sockeye) is on and screaming down the river past about a hundred lines, the whole thing becomes high comedy. Comedy, that is, if you aren't in the middle of it all with a hopeless snarl in your line and someone else's size 6/0 hook in your earlobe.

A Soggy Fishing Camp, Southwestern Alaska by Tully Stroud

THE FISHING CAMP

Fishermen do many odd things in the name of having fun. Prominent among these peculiar activities is the fishing trip to a location where living conditions give new meaning to the word squalor. And great premiums are usually paid for the privilege of forsaking even the most elementary of creature comforts.

These dedicated, but arguably deranged, trout chasers are enjoying a drying out period after six straight days of rain in the Alaskan bush. The weather posed no obstacle to the fishing, of course, but it definitely put a damper on campfires. Worse, a mess tent with more holes than canvas made evening poker games impossible.

All this may not sound serious, but it strikes a blow to the very essence of a fishing trip. After the last cast is made and darkness forces a retreat to the fire, the sport continues. More fish are hooked and lost over the beers and the card games than are ever encountered in the streams. Not because fishermen are liars, but because every strike is relived and every pool refished until the imagination runs amuck.

Fishing without the camaraderie of the camp is like a river without fish—the water's there, but the heart and soul are missing.

Alaskan Trout Arsenal by R. Valentine Atkinson

IN DEFENSE OF THE COST OF FISHING

Never get suckered into defending the cost of your fishing habit on a cost per pound basis. It'll only embarrass or depress you. The only measure that makes sense at all is the cost per cast. By my calculation, the CPC for a seven-day fishing trip can be as little as a half cent and rarely over a quarter for even the exotic destinations. Very reasonable, indeed. So, if you're long on effort and short on results, remember that the more you cast, the cheaper it gets.

Lonesome Lake, Popo Agie Primitive Area, Wind River Range, Wyoming by Pat O'Hara

HIGH COUNTRY

A surprising number of trout fishermen have never left the more readily accessible streams and lakes to venture into the world of the high country. We needn't go all the way to Alaska to find trout in a tundra setting. With just a little extra effort, we can find plenty of fish in the lakes that lie in the highest life zones of many of the national parks and other public lands in the "Lower 48."

From the spring thaw through the first snows, the high country displays a kaleidoscope of colors and contrasts so beautiful, it's easy to forget we're there to fish.

The Hatch by R. Valentine Atkinson

MOSQUITOES

This picture is neither out of focus nor shot through a dirty lens. The air is just beclouded by harmless aquatic insects of the type that fishermen's dreams are made of.

But, let's be completely honest. The most reliable and copious hatches of aquatic insects that seem to be found along much of the summertime trout water in North America—at least the streams I wind up on—are *not* mayflies, caddisflies, or stoneflies. They are more likely to be positively vicious little pests apparently put on this earth for the sole purpose of transforming an otherwise perfect day into purgatory.

Mosquitoes are loathsome vermin. Period. No apologies. I don't care what role they may play in Nature's grand scheme, I want them gone forever!

Modern science has finally provided us with such potent repellents that (so far at least) the little !@#$%¢&**s can't poke through with their nasty little probes. So instead, they settle for psychological warfare and circle noisily around our heads by the billions until the dementia inducing drone drives us to cover.

[In the interest of full and fair disclosure, the editors insist I point out that blaming a few bugs for a trout fisherman's insanity is somewhat akin to blaming plankton for the sinking of the Titanic.]

Gibbon River, Yellowstone National Park, Wyoming by R. Valentine Atkinson

GOING BACK

Fishing is one of those magic things in life that can not only make time stand still, but go backward as well. Not just hours or days, but entire lifetimes. We can stand in the same stream at eighty that we waded at ten and lose every minute that cluttered the years between.

Arctic Char (Salvelinus alpinus*), Southwestern Alaska by Lani Waller*

THE BULLY

Arctic char are the ruffians of trout and salmondom. (Being char, they are neither trout nor salmon, and this confused identity may contribute to their ill-mannered behavior.) If these fish were birds, they'd be brazen crows or bluejays. Maybe cuckoos. If they were mammals, they'd be junkyard dogs.

Like the rainbow trout, arctic char rely on a late summer feast of salmon roe to fatten them up and tide them over through the long Alaskan winter. But whereas the more polite rainbow is usually content to bide its time finning expectantly downstream from the salmon redds and waiting for nature to take its course, the char is apt to tire of the waiting game and give nature a kick-start. Targeting a ripe female salmon, a char will often take dead aim and ram her in the side at full speed, causing a premature delivery and yielding a stream full of salmon eggs.

Just imagine how the poor salmon must feel. Up to that point, she has battled the ravages of rapid sexual maturity, fought her way up rapids and waterfalls, and dodged bears and gill nets—only to reach her destination and have some thug of a distant cousin show up and play bumper pool with her belly.

Not nice. But it's part of nature's way. Better observed than tampered with. In defense of the bullies, it should be said that there's not a single report of a salmon run ever being wiped out or even seriously endangered by schools of kamikaze char. The same defense, of course, could be accurately applied to bears, otters, ospreys, eagles, seals and virtually all the world's fish chasers—save only one.

Liberating Bugs from the Chardonnay by Tully Stroud

BAIT & SWITCH

"Freak coincidence, my foot!" my wife Patricia complained one day after one salami sandwich too many. "This was all just a cruel bait-and-switch and a lousy trick. Just listen and tell me I'm wrong. First, you hook me by taking me to a gorgeous river in a meadow full of flowers. You lovingly show me how to fish. Then, you set the hook a little deeper by paying constant attention to me while I'm learning, and to clinch it, you even cook me a couple of gourmet streamside meals. Naturally I decide this fishing stuff is fun—just like you planned."

She was on a roll, and it would seem that I was squarely in her path.

"Then once I'm addicted to what I *think* is trout fishing, I find out what these trips are *really* like. Now you only take me to places where the bugs bite me and drink more of my wine than I do. Instead of holding my hand in a field full of flowers, you go off alone and fish for 14 straight hours—leaving me on a stream so brushy I need a chain saw to reach the water. The brush doesn't really matter much though, because the wind is always blowing 40 miles an hour and I couldn't cast even if I did reach the river. And worse—suddenly all the food on these trips comes from cans, lunchmeat containers, or potato chip bags. Nice job, but you'd better sink some more effort into this whole fishing togetherness thing pretty fast, because your original investment is tapped out!"

Hmmmmmm. Until that moment, I'd never really thought of fishing as a passbook savings account. I think what she was really trying to say was that just by hitting a few more of the dreamy streams with restaurants nearby, I could get away with fishing a lot more. The greater the investment, the greater the return. The concept is mind boggling.

Lamar River, Yellowstone National Park, Wyoming by Pat O'Hara

TROUT ENVIRONS

An icthyologist might tell us that the lack of environmental adaptability by trout and salmon has put them in a rather perilous corner from a survival standpoint. After all, around 20 percent of all vertebrate species are freshwater fishes, yet less than half of one percent of those are salmonids. Their particular requirements for reproduction and survival have left them in retreat as the cold, clear water they need has grown ever scarcer since the last ice age. To greatly worsen matters, man has been monumentally unkind to much of their habitat.

Environmental choosiness may be a Darwinian peril, but it is also the real magnet of trout fishing. The niche of nature in which these fish continue to do quite well, thank you, puts them squarely in the midst of what many of us think is the most beautiful country on earth. Would trout fishing be the same if trout had been as adaptive as catfish?

Gibbon River, Yellowstone National Park, Wyoming by Kitty Pearson-Vincent

SUNSET

The last hour of daylight on the summertime trout stream is just about as good as our world gets. One sunset, and the healing goosebumps that go with it, can suddenly undo the annealing of our souls, slowly forged by the daily fires of urban living.

Merced River, Yosemite National Park, California by Larry Ulrich

FALL

Autumn is a bittersweet time for trout fishermen. If the winter ahead is a time for antici-
pating the seasons to come, then fall is a time for quiet
reflection on seasons past. A time for pensive thoughts
about things done and undone. About roads not taken
and rivers not fished.

Autumn nostalgia is as involuntary as a heartbeat,
brought on by internal forces as old as the species. And
no amount of planned winter fishing can allay the sen-
timentality. Another season is gone, and it's a little sad.

But just as certainly as autumn marks a passing, it
also foretells and assures a coming. Each leaf that drifts
by us in the stream has given way so that a new leaf
might replace it. For a new and better season to come,
an old season must go.

This coming and going is one of the things that makes
rivers so special. The water that passes by with each

moment, like the moment itself, will never do so again. Though we may fish the same river for a hundred years, we will never really fish the same river twice.

Wait a minute! We're fishermen here, not second-rate poets. The pretext for all this reflective time by ourselves is still *fishing*. Autumn is indeed a time for a thankful look around and back, but it's also a time to cram in as many hours on the stream as possible before bidding temporary farewell to our favorite pastime.

And what fishing it is. The trout are fat from feasting. Insect hatches are plentiful. Water conditions are perfect. Summer crowds have gone home, and we can be alone on the stream at last. ("Fall" for the trout fisherman, incidentally, doesn't wait for the equinox, but begins sometime in mid-September when all the schools have returned to session.)

But which stream?

The options are legion. The steelhead and king salmon runs of the Pacific Coast and Great Lakes. The big lake-run rainbows in Alaska. The fall browns in Montana, Michigan, and Alberta. The old reliable stream just out of town.

Thankfully, not every trout fisherman covets the same waters or the same fish. It's virtually impossible to get even two fishermen to agree on anything so theoretical as the ideal fall fishing trip. Such debates, while great fun, are largely rhetorical anyway, because most of us can seldom afford the time and money it takes to reach the fabled waters. Streams like the Sustut, Bow, Lower Talarik, Big Horn, and Pere Marquette are not in everyone's backyard. That the fisherman can't reach the stream of his dreams as often as he'd like isn't so important. The important thing is that he can dream.

For the dreams to continue, there must be streams left to covet. Man has proven time and again that even the mightiest of rivers is perishable. The smaller streams can be downright ephemeral. We've used most of the world's rivers to light our cities, quench our thirst, water crops and lawns, float logs to mill, relocate waste, control floods, open flood plains to development, and provide lakes for recreation. The riverine casualties are countless.

Fishermen know well that the battle is bigger than trout fishing. The struggle to save trout is inseparable from the larger struggle to preserve and restore our rivers and lakes. If the latter efforts are successful, trout will piggyback their way to a prosperous future. If efforts to save and clean up our waters fail, no amount of concern about the fish in them will matter in the end.

In 1968, the Wild and Scenic Rivers Act became law, and we river lovers rejoiced. With such a congressional mandate, we expected that by the year 1990, more than 200 of our finest rivers would be protected

*"Thankfully, not every trout fisherman covets the
same waters or the same fish. It's virtually impossible
to get even two fishermen to agree on anything so
theoretical as the ideal fall fishing trip."*

in a national Wild and Scenic Rivers System. Eighteen years later, rivers
numbering less than a third of that goal are protected—and they were
the easy pickings. Future additions to the system, if they come at all,
will be fiscally expensive. Short-term financial costs of land acquisition
for river protection are easy to measure and easy prey for the budget
axe. The longer-term social and psychic benefits of those expenditures
don't lend themselves so easily to articulation in financial terms. Instead, appeals on behalf of these benefits often have to rely on our
instinctive sense of right and wrong. In times of budget deficit woes,
that makes river protection funds a tough sell indeed.

Sonofagun! Just when it looks as if the battle is lost, there materializes
a veritable explosion of grass roots river conservation movements. Co-
alitions of private conservation groups, the business community, and
state and local governments across the country are taking creative ap-
proaches that work. The National Park Service is lending valuable technical assistance. These increasingly common team efforts recognize
that, while the rivers themselves cross a variety of public and private
jurisdictional boundaries (a fact that has made river protection a nightmare), a broad interest in the health of the streams does exist. Increased
use of such techniques as tax incentives, zoning, and direct acquisition
(by nonpublic funds) has been effective. "Home" rivers across the
country, which could never have been saved at the federal level, are
being protected.

Why all the concern over a little water? It's a lot more than the self-
interest of fishermen and other conservationists. The root of this concern is a nagging knowledge carried somewhere in our genes that we
really ought to leave some of the natural world alone. Rivers, great or
small, can swallow up our cares, and like other works of Nature, can
be the catalysts that provide a truer sense of scale and a perspective
born of seeing our own humble limits surpassed by even the simplest
of natural wonders. They are places of retreat where we can find tran-
quility—and often a better understanding of what does and doesn't
matter in the great scheme of things.

Spey Casting, Bulkley River, British Columbia by Kitty Pearson-Vincent

CHARLES

Charles was old, and he walked with a slow, deliberate shuffle that favored his severely arthritic knee. His quick eyes and furrowed face hinted at a wisdom that was quickly confirmed when he spoke.

His wife of 40 years had died two years before, and Charles was alone. His days were spent writing, fishing, spinning tales of his many travels, and humming repetitively the same four notes of a Brandenberg concerto. He had never seen even one television program ("Though I understand they have some very fine nature programs now," he admitted).

A group of us met Charles on a steelheading trip to British Columbia. He had enchanted us all before we even wet a line. Watching him struggle along on stiffened land legs made us fear for his safety in the swift currents of the rocky stream—but he surprised us. With only a staff and a lot of common sense, he waded deeper and more effectively than the younger members of the group, and in a week of the trickiest wading, no one saw him stumble once.

When it came to fishing, Charles really held class for all. He read the water impeccably and covered it deftly with his flies. When the week was over, Charles had outfished us all—by plenty. But he left us feeling pretty good about our years of fishing ahead. And very aware of how much we had yet to grow, in fishing and in life.

FALL

Still Life of Defeat by Tully Stroud

THE LEGEND

Be honest now. Is there a fisherman alive who hasn't secretly fantasized about becoming a fishing legend? An honest-to-goodness celebrity who could walk into a restaurant, bar, or tackle shop in, say, West Yellowstone, Montana or Roscoe, New York and put an immediate hush over an assembled crowd of fishermen?

"Wow, that's Double Haul Stroud!" they'd whisper. "He's the best fly fisherman alive." Or something like that.

After a lifetime of chasing after merely mortal trout in a very mortal fashion, I finally decided it was time to overcome my well-earned anonymity. So, seeking fishing immortality, I headed for the fabled steelhead waters of British Columbia's Babine River in search of the world's record rainbow trout on a fly. And the rest, as they say, is history.

Today, I can probably walk into any establishment in nearby Smithers, B.C. and hear the crowd hush.

"Good grief, that's Slip-knot Stroud," they'd chuckle. "Can you believe he'd show up around here again after becoming the first guy in history to lose *three* entire flylines in *three* steelhead on *three* straight days—with 200 yards of backing left on his reel each time? The moron couldn't even tie a simple knot in *three* tries. You know, until he stumbled along, the record for lost flylines was zero."

Somehow, I think I'd rather be anonymous.

Madison River, Yellowstone National Park, Wyoming by Larry Dech

THE MADISON

Put a campfire, idle time, and a few fishermen together, and it's inevitable that experiences will be shared and comparisons made. One topic that recurs is the game of naming the most beautiful river. Not the best fishing river, mind you, but simply the most beautiful. It's not a debate, just a way to pass the time.

One river (actually a river system) gets more than a random share of votes from new friends and old alike. The Madison in Yellowstone National Park, along with its parent streams the Gibbon and the Firehole, make the list almost every time. Taken together, they glide through some of the finest scenery in all the world. Wildlife teems alongside, and the rivers themselves are absolutely classic trout water—crystal clear, cold, and full of fish.

Some of those fish are pretty big. Unfortunately for me, they grew to their considerable size by avoiding mistakes and learning when to keep their mouths shut. I never minded much. If I were told I'd be skunked, but could pick the place of my choice, I'd probably choose a meadow somewhere along one of these streams. The fishing would just be a thin excuse for being there.

Fisherman's Gothic by R. Valentine Atkinson

FISHERMAN'S GOTHIC

The joys of trout fishing come not only from basking in our own successes,
but in savoring the uncontained exuberance our fishing companions show
when sharing those happy moments with us.

Jock Scott by Kris Lee

THE ATLANTIC SALMON FLY

Feather-winged Atlantic salmon flies, those blue-blooded holdovers from the Victorian era, seem to appeal to a fish's sense of good taste and decorum. Though now made of look-alike substitutes, these flies were once feathered by exotic fowl from the far corners of the British Empire and beyond. Toucan, blue chatterer, Indian crow, speckled bustard, florican bustard, macaw, and jungle cock were just a few of the many contributors.

The master tiers of these showpieces are artists, and their painstaking attention to craftsmanship and detail rivals the makers of fine cane rods.

Don't be fooled by the good looks of these flies. They also catch fish—and very big ones at that. Not just Atlantic salmon, but Pacific salmon and steelhead too. There is, however, a big problem with using these beauties. If you lose one, it'll break your heart.

Brown Trout (Salmo trutta) by Curt Ries

GAMBLERS

The most seriously afflicted streamside gamblers can turn an otherwise peaceful fishing trip into a bookkeeper's nightmare. They'll sit beside the lantern playing cards for money until the last opponent nods off in his bug dope. Then they'll sit around the breakfast campfire offering a wide variety of sporting propositions for the day's fishing until someone takes the bait. Five bucks for the first fish, five bucks for the most fish, ten bucks for the biggest fish. It never stops, and they won't let up until they're thrown a bone.

It has been my extreme financial misfortune to know such a person. An otherwise fine fellow and consummate fisherman, Jim needs a good bet to get him going each day the way the rest of us need a cup of coffee. Once hands are shaken, he's on the river without rest until he's sure he's won or he can't see to fish any longer. He seldom loses.

This man once talked me into betting with him at a buck an inch on brown trout, with no fish under twenty inches counting. Since we'd both been skunked the prior day, I figured what the heck—it'll shut him up and it won't cost me a dime.

I worked nervously at fishing all that day under a pressure that took the fun out of it. Nevertheless, I strutted proudly into camp at dusk with a magnificent 4½-pound, 23-inch brown—only to find I'd lost $42.50.

That was the very day I converted to catch-and-release fishing, and I've had a clearer conscience and fatter wallet ever since. These gambler types, I've discovered, will seek easier prey rather than take a gentleman at his word where a wager is at stake.

Yellowstone River, Montana by David Stoecklein

LUCK

Most fishermen make their own luck. A chosen few, I am reluctantly convinced, are simply born with it.

A number of years ago, I introduced a friend to trout fishing. On the long drive to the river, he told me of a trans-Sierra hike he'd just completed. According to his story, he had worn blisters the size of golf balls on both feet when, with more than a week of miserable hiking still ahead, he rounded a bend in the trail and came upon a pair of canvas sneakers in just his size.

"A fluke," he said.

"A lie," I thought, not realizing he had been congenitally blessed with good fortune.

When we got to the river, I told him to make a few practice casts before heading on downstream to a less crowded spot. He stood on the bank of the most heavily fished pool in the river and hooked and landed a big fat brown trout on his second cast. While I was still shaking my head in disbelief, he said, "Hey, do they all have this funny tag?"

I read the small green plastic tag attached to a fin. It went something like this:

Return this tag to the Department
of Fish and Game for a $10 Reward.

I had fished that river for half a lifetime and had never seen a single tagged fish, much less one with a bounty on its head.

We are still good friends, but I haven't been fishing with the man since. It's just too depressing.

Trout Unlimited Pioneer George Griffith, Au Sable River, Michigan by Larry Dech

PRESERVATION

At one time, only the rich or those lucky enough to live in the right place could hope to catch a big trout. Now, not just because of increased accessibility, but also because dedicated fishermen spoke out, almost any fisherman has a wide choice of places that offer an honest shot at a trout of two pounds or more.

Quality trout fishing in America has been preserved through decades of hard work by a lot of people who have cared. These individuals, groups, and guardians of the public trust have put forth articulate resistance to thwart man's seemingly never-ending assault on trout habitats. As a direct result, trout fishing today is arguably better than ever.

What will it be like fifty years from now? Continuing and deadly serious challenges, such as acid rain, silting, and new dams should keep us busy until we pass the baton to our great grandchildren. If we drop it, "better than ever" will almost surely take a heartbreaking turn for the worse.

Man with Steelhead, Flat River, Michigan by Larry Dech

HERO SHOTS

The smile is easy to understand, but why is this happy fisherman sliming himself (and risking hurting the fish in the process) by holding his soon-to-be released trophy in a bear hug? Wouldn't it be easier and more pleasant for the fish to cup him gently under the belly with both hands and lift him horizontally for the photographer? Still, such caressing poses are so common among shots of fishermen with big fish (known as "hero shots") that I suspected there was a reason. With little experience in such situations, I was sentenced to wonder.

Then—in an improbable feat that proved the fishing corollary to the monkeys and typewriters theory—I actually *caught* a big fish. Naturally, before I freed the 38-inch steelhead buck, the event had to be immortalized on film. So, I slipped both hands carefully under him and lifted. The startled fish writhed with all the slithering torque of a speeding anaconda and fell back into the water with me spread atop him. Three more tries met the same fate. Then, I remembered the hero shots I'd puzzled over. Wrapping both arms tightly around him, I stood up, the shutter clicked and moments later the fish was back in the river, free of the whole indignity.

And the mystery was solved. How do you hold a fish for a hero shot? Any way you can!

Armstrong's Spring Creek, Montana by Charles F. Waterman

MONTANA

Poll a thousand trout fishermen from coast to coast. Ask them to list three places they've either fished or intend to fish "someday." I'll bet you my entire collection of marabou muddlers that more than 90 percent of the lists will include the word "Montana."

Most of us fishing types grew up devoting many of our winter evenings to wistful reading about rivers with names like Madison, Yellowstone, Big Hole, Beaverhead, and Gallatin. About spring creeks like Armstrong's and Nelson's. Lately, we've added the Big Horn to the roll. Between Montana and neighboring Idaho, Wyoming, and Yellowstone National Park, it's all there for the trout fisherman.

If, for some incomprehensible reason, you want a break from the fishing for a bit, you can always take in some of the area's colorful sights. Places like Robber's Roost, Buffalo Jump, Chief Joseph Pass, and Custer Battlefield. Yep folks, this is also the Wild West—and out here, it ain't even dead yet! Why, not long ago they almost had a shooting war on the outskirts of Dillon, Montana between a rancher and—you'd better sit down for this one—a bunch of irate *trout fishermen* and river guides. Things are peaceful now. With the Montana State Supreme Court and Montana Legislature playing the role of Cavalry, the rights of fishermen to fish in peace (subject to some reasonable restrictions) are hopefully etched in stone. And the guys in the white hats can finally go to sleep with their boots off ... for a while at least.

Enchantment Basin, Alpine Lakes Wilderness, Washington by Pat O'Hara

SILENCE

Silence. Stark, bludgeoning silence. Have you ever heard it? You notice it immediately when you arrive from the city. It's so quiet that you can't sleep. Then you begin to adjust until, after a day or so, every click of the fishing reel and each snap of a twig becomes an annoying intrusion. Being part of this kind of stillness gets to the heart of what fishing is really about.

Beaverkill River, New York by Kris Lee

NO-KILL FISHING

Wild trout are an exhaustible resource. Once we've proven to ourselves that we can catch fish, we eventually lose the need, and the will, to bring home trophies to prove it. With the wisdom of age (increasingly found in the young as well) we come to understand that the chase itself is the real object of the game, and that the careful release of a conquered fish is much more satisfying to the psyche than gutting or filleting the corpse. This holds true wherever we fish and not just where the law requires it. When we adopt this "no-kill" attitude, the quarry takes on its proper role as the goal of an unending quest. Such a quarry has value to us only in the stream.

Big Horn River, Montana by Tom Montgomery

LATE FALL FISHING

For the fisherman willing to put up with those minor physical discomforts that come when the air temperature plunges far below that of the river, late fall is the time to fish trout streams just about anywhere. Long, hot days of summer yield to the crisp days of autumn just as sun-loving fishermen yield to anglers who gladly accept the little extra pain to get the considerable extra solitude.

Besides, where is it written that the clouds of frozen breath encircling us in late October are any worse than clouds of mosquitoes in July? We can always find warmth by a cheery fire or with a credit card at the nearest motel, but no currency or plastic can buy us a lonely piece of the river when the skies are friendlier.

Swauk Creek, Washington by Pat O'Hara

WINTER

Let's face it. Winter these days is only a state of mind among trout fishermen—more an old habit that's hard to break than a governmental or climatic ban on fishing.

Generations of Americans grew accustomed to bidding a temporary farewell to trout fishing as autumn leaves brightened, fell, and drifted past in the stream. Spouses and families rejoiced with the legal closing of the season, viewing it as an opportunity to become reacquainted with the loved one they lost when the season opened in spring. Some fishermen—I'm told of, but have never actually met—welcome winter as a sort of forced "drying out" period. A chance to replant themselves in reality and get rational before the next season. A time to spend with those people and things so long neglected. A time to clear the fish-besotted brain and guilt-ridden conscience.

Winter was once a quiet time to sit in front of the fire and look over our tackle after the long season of use and abuse. With patience, even fondness, we cleaned our lines and examined them for nicks. We replaced short and wind-knotted leaders, remembering how we squeezed every possible minute of fishing into those last evenings of fall. We cleaned and oiled our reels. We buffed rods back to their original lustre. We tied flies. We made long lists of needed equipment in anticipation of the arrival of the new fishing catalogs. We studied maps and planned trips.

Not anymore! Some sinister force has been at work, scheming to obliterate our wintertime reunion with the rest of the world and to deny us the luxury of fondling our beloved tackle.

Year round trout season! Egad, even the mention of it must strike horror into the hearts of fishing widows and widowers everywhere. Yet quietly and inexorably, the 365-day trout season has caught on. Nearly half the states no longer close the season at all, and several others have very short closures or close only selected waters, leaving at least some fishing available throughout the year.

Still, winter trout fishing on most North American waters does demand a tolerance for cold and a zealous resolve that many uninformed observers mistake for outright dementia. This unfortunate misconception is only heightened by media hype over a few extremists, like winter steelheaders or the guy who spends his winter days and nights huddled in a frigid cave (overlooking Utah's Flaming Gorge Reservoir) between missions in search of the world's record brown trout. It's a bum rap for most of us more typical, warmblooded trout chasers who wouldn't put up with that kind of cave dwelling for more than a week or so at a time. Unless, of course, the cave came with satellite T.V. and a hot shower.

No, the season may be open, but clearly, winter trout fishing in the U.S. isn't for everyone. Yet, even those fishermen strong-willed enough to pass up the opportunity to test their limits of endurance for cold are being tempted away from the livingroom fires by still another wintertime opportunity. It's called summer.

It seems that the seeds thoughtfully sewn by our forefathers have taken root and are bearing incredible fruit south of the equator—where January means T-shirts and sunburns. Originally void of all trout, rivers in the Southern Hemisphere have been enriched with the progeny of fish that once swam in Europe and the United States. Some of the early efforts to introduce fish below zero latitude entailed transporting fertilized eggs in the ice-filled holds of British ships. The ice melted too quickly on the first couple of tries, but the unshakable determination of frustrated trout chasers living "down under" eventually paid off.

Now the fishing media deluges us with opportunities to take out another mortgage on the house, leave the family behind, and head for

"The mere temptation of winter trout fishing
has perhaps induced more psychic confusion among
trout fishermen than anything since the
invention of the fish hook."

the likes of Tazmania, New Zealand, and Argentina. Wouldn't January be more exciting if we traded in our snow shovels for a graphite fly rod and headed for Tierra del Fuego? There we could spend a double daylight shift leaning at roughly a 45° angle into the routine gale-force winds south of the Straits of Magellan—fishing between gusts for giant searun brown trout. The fact that it may be several days between gusts would only serve to heighten the anticipation and make lulls all the sweeter.

Or maybe we could reduce our chances of returning home to find the locks changed if we cashed in the IRAs and took a family Christmas vacation to New Zealand. A sightseeing/shopping/dining trip with a "little" fishing thrown in now and then? Plausible. Tempting. Well okay, obsessive.

Alas, endless trout fishing is a lot like endless football. It's exactly like endless football—too much of a great thing.

We *need* time to reflect on the past season and prepare for the next. How can we, if there's no season? When will we have time to sit in our warm homes and play with our cherished rods and reels in the glow of a cozy winter fire? When will we feel the aching thrill of anticipation that builds to an explosive crescendo before the gun finally sounds next spring? When indeed.

But what a torment. It's like dangling a fly in front of a frog. The mere temptation of winter trout fishing has perhaps induced more psychic confusion among trout fishermen than anything since the invention of the fish hook. Psychiatrists and divorce lawyers love it. I think they may have secretly sponsored it.

I guess it really is nice to have options, though. Isn't it? After all, we're grown ups—we can resist temptations and make intelligent choices. So winter is simply whatever we want it to be. All things considered, most of us still just want it to be over. Or do we? Damn, I wish I could make up my mind!

Madison River, Montana by Larry Dech

THE REAL TROUT FISHERMAN

Winter trout fishing above the sunbelt is not for the timid. It calls for a zealous dedication that a lot of us warm-blooded creatures can't reach down and find. So if you want to find a *real* trout fisherman, go to a northern stream in January or February. When you see something in or along the river that moves and isn't completely white, you've found what you are looking for. There are *no* pretenders afoot at these times.

Queets River, Olympic National Park, Washington by Pat O'Hara

THE WINTER STEELHEADER

The poet Robert Service once observed that "There's a race of men that don't fit in." In the genteel sport of trout and salmon fishing, that race would have to be represented by the winter steelheaders. Hands down. These guys are fishing's answer to duck hunters, only worse.

The steelheader gets up in the freezing predawn darkness to reach the river by first light. There he stands, shivering in the rain or snow all day, waist deep in icy water, hoping against hope that there's a fish somewhere in the area. If there is a fish around, he must try, against long odds, to make it strike by casting squarely in front of its unseen and apathetic nose. If this improbable feat is accomplished, he must then pray that some sixth sense will tell him precisely when the nearly imperceptible event has occurred so that he may set the hook before the fish spits it out in disgust.

Remember now, steelheaders do this in the name of recreation, *voluntarily* and *repeatedly* throughout the long winter. Incredible as it may seem, these people are permitted to be at large in society, marry, and even to reproduce themselves (if they can find the time).

Still, it must be confessed that this odd race is usually spoken of in curiously envious tones, even admiration, whenever the rest of us less dedicated fanatics meet to discuss our obsession.

Little Wood River, Idaho by Terry Ring

HEROES

When you chance upon a person whose idols as a kid more or less match his idols thirty or so years later, you've probably found someone permanently stuck in that blissful childhood state when all of life was a Saturday matinee and heroes were deities. *Please,* don't wake him up.

The other boys I knew longed to be another Ted Williams or President Eisenhower. I wanted to be Lee Wulff or Ray Bergman. ("Who?" they'd ask, having their doubts.) The rest of the kids compared autographs and swapped baseball cards. I reread my most cherished possession: a letter from Joe Brooks himself thanking me for some trout flies I'd dared to send him.

Today little has changed. The letter from Joe lies encased in lucite on my coffee table, and I'm still trying to work up the nerve to write to Lee. I'm not ashamed to say I haven't "grown" an inch on these important matters. I *have* added a few new heroes to the list—all fishermen and fishing writers, naturally. I've also warmed up considerably to Ike and Ted too since I found out they'd really rather have been fishing.

Fall River, California by Larry Ulrich

THE COUNTENANCE OF STREAMS

Trout fishing waters are so varied that there are streams to satisfy any and every fisherman's mood. Big streams and little streams. Rough and tumble freestone streams. Calm, meandering ones. Streams with rainbow trout, brown trout, cutthroat trout, or brook trout—and streams with all of them. Dammed streams and undammed streams. Streams with deep pool after deep pool and streams with barely a pause between riffles or white water. Streams surrounded by pines, alders, birch, aspens, or sagebrush. Mountain streams and meadow streams. Country streams and even a few city streams. Streams with big fish and streams with small fish. Streams in warming sunlight and streams in deep, shadowed canyons and forests.

No two streams are alike, and trout fishing would suffer if it were otherwise.

Madison River, Montana by Larry Dech

THE SHORT WADER

Successful wading— which to most of us is any wading that doesn't result in a dunking—is based on a very reliable law of physics. Put simply, this law states that for any body partially immersed in water, it is the weight of the mass *above* the water that causes the essentially weightless mass *below* the water to remain in place on the bottom. The practical implication of this to fishermen is that no matter how big our heads, if we wade in deep enough, we will simply float away.

Well now, even the most casual observer can see that this unalterable fact stacks the deck heavily in favor of the tall fisherman. Yet I know one short fisherman who steadfastly refuses to accept his handicap. Preston is easily the most fearless wader I know, even though he sometimes needs a boost to use a pay phone. His ground-hugging stature and aggressive wading has made him by far the most accomplished swimmer among my group of fishing cronies.

Over the years, the rest of us have learned to fish upstream from Preston, so that he doesn't disturb our pools as he comes bobbing and sidestroking down the river. Water ballet it isn't, but he's perfected this odd stroke—with wading shoes in one hand and rod in the other— to a near artform and even learned to fish while doing it. We once watched incredulously as he scrambled ashore after a rather remarkable performance and reeled in forty feet of line with a two-pound rainbow trout on the end.

So much for the practical implications of physics on the determined fisherman.

Winter Steelheader, Alder Creek, California by R. Valentine Atkinson

THE ILLUSION

It would appear that not all winter fishing scenes in North America are set in white. In what he insists is an unretouched photograph, Valentine Atkinson has captured one of trout fishing's most unlikely scenes: 1) a windless, rainless January day on the northern California coast; 2) *green* fields with grazing cows; and 3) a winter steelheader.

C'mon Valentine. We'll accept the cows and verdant pastures. Even the almost friendly skies. But a winter steelheader? We all know these anglers are invisible to cameras—no doubt for the same reason they are thought to be invisible in mirrors.

Anyone who knows him will tell you that Mr. Atkinson is a man of unimpeachable integrity. But alas, he's also a fisherman. Accordingly, his photo is reproduced here without any representations, expressed or implied, as to its authenticity.

Little Blackfoot River, Montana by Pat O'Hara

TOO MANY RIVERS LEFT TO FISH

When you're feeling a little down or simply old and spent, consider the advice once given to me by a lifelong fishing friend at a time (many casts ago) when I was so ill that others were telling me to hurry up and bequeath my fishing rods.

"You aren't done yet," he scolded me. "There are too many rivers left to fish."
Amen.